#MAKEAMERICAGREATAGAIN

Donald Trump & The Political Campaign

This book is dedicated to the men and women who make America great.

Contents

Biography

Donald John Trump is a billionaire real estate developer, author and a famous TV personality in the United States of America. Born in 1946 to Mr. Frederick and Mrs. Mary Trump as their fourth child of five children, Donald Trump was sent to be educated in the New York Military Academy at the age of 13. After graduating in 1964, he attended the Wharton School of Finance at the University of Pennsylvania to obtain a degree in economics.

After his successful graduation from the University of Pennsylvania in 1968, Donald Trump joined his father's company, Elizabeth Trump & Sons, which he later named as the Trump organization after he was transferred its control. Trump experienced ups and downs in his business while he expanded his company and acquired wealth and public recognition in the United States. Purchasing the Plaza Hotel in New York and the acquisition of the ownership of Miss Universe Organization are some of his well-known endeavors. Donald Trump gained popularity when he became a joint partner with the NBC (National Broadcasting Cooperation) in 2003 and produced and hosted a reality show named, The Apprentice.

His first marriage was to Ivana Zelnickova in 1977 from which he had three children. The couple got divorced when Ivana learned about the love affair Trump was having with an American actress by the name Marla Maples. Later, Trump married Marla Maples in 1993 with whom he had a child two months prior to their marriage. Donald Trump is currently married to Melania Knauss whom he married in 2005 after the divorce from his second marriage.

On 16th June, 2015 Donald Trump announced his run for US President 2016 from the Republican Party and is one of the most controversial and discussed candidates to date.

#MAKEAMERICAGREATAGAIN

DONALD J. TRUMP

The Political Views

Immigration

Ending the relationship with NBC

NBC which had a long standing alliance of 11 years with Donald Trump decided to cut their ties in June 2015. The reason behind this action based solely on the remarks Trump made about the Mexican immigrants in the United States.

The partnership between NBC and Donald Trump started off in 2003 with Trump being the Executive producer and host of the reality show, The Apprentice. This alliance grew with the success of the show up to this date. But NBC stated that the statement Trump made saying the immigrants to United States of America included criminals and rapists made them distance from Trump and later faced the pressure to cut ties.

NBC also mentioned that they will end all business relationships with Trump and will no longer air the "Miss Universe" or "Miss USA" pageants by the Miss Universe Organization which is under the ownership of Trump. NBC also noted that Donald Trump will not continue as the host of The Apprentice due to his potential Presidential candidacy was said by him.

After this announcement was made, Donald Trump blasted NBC saying that if the media channel is weak and foolish not to understand the illegal immigration issue and the unfair trade deals being made with Mexico, then he will let the contract violation by the closure of Miss Universe and Miss USA pageants be determined in court. He also added that NBC supports liars like Brian Williams and not the people who express their realistic ideas.

Trump mentioned that he had a great relationship with the media company but their views on immigration is much different to his. His concerns were expressed saying the illegal immigrants commit great amount of crimes and it must be stopped now for the betterment of the country. He further stated to NBC that he will not change his stance on this matter.

Building a wall separating USA and Mexico

Donald Trump, a business man and the GOP front runner appeared in Harrisburg in April, 2016 to speak for his followers. The crowd was visibly excited to see the Republican Presidential aspirant in person.

He unequivocally made it known to the loud cheers that his government if elected, would build the wall separating the US from Mexico. Peoples' excitement and appraisal for the statement was evident as each time it was mentioned, he got the loudest cheers.

The Presidential aspirant told the crowd in Harrisburg that he would never hesitate to build the wall and that after he is through with it, it would be called the "Trump Wall". This triggered even much louder applause from the audience.

Another wave of applause ensued when he declared that he would create more job opportunities. He promised to revitalize all jobs, even from Mexico which he said had continued to take away the jobs in USA. People, in their quest for good jobs promised to cast their votes to him. Many people also confessed that his personality was the type they needed for a president as he's capable of creating an abundance of job opportunities.

Trump also promised to welcome immigrants but unveiled that for that to happen, all immigration must be legal and legitimate. Moreover, Trump said he was ready to forgo business deals as to ignite good leadership to the White House. He also made it known that he would work against Hillary Clinton even though some people were still confused on who to vote for. Trump maintained that he was the best candidate for the post.

Introducing waterboarding and enhanced interrogation techniques

Donald Trump, the Republican presidential candidate greeted everyone happily after addressing the American Israel Public Affairs Committee. He said that the U.S ought to use waterboarding and other strict questioning techniques to interrogate miscreants. He also called for good security in the border after the Brussels attack. He said that the authorities should ensure they get firsthand information to ensure that further attacks could be prevented.

He further advised that more and sensitive information could be obtained from torture because according to him torture could produce sound guide. Waterboarding, being a tactic of pouring water over someone's face as to make interrogation was abolished by President Barack Obama. Trump hereby backed its renewal because he thought it could bring better security.

He however, called for a thorough check in the mosques as to prevent further attacks since the Muslims seemed instrumental to the number of attacks that had always busted in the country. He also called for tightening of the border to ensure that illegal immigrants do not migrate into the country as well as temporarily ban the Muslims from entering the country.

Trump also doubted the U.S role in the North Treaty Organization and called for the use of austerity measure on the defense alliance. Trump went further into devising a means of winning the Republican presidential nomination which was aimed at countering his party setbacks. He also called for the building of walls following his recent suggestion of banning Muslims from entering the country.

Making the position on worker's visa clear

Donald Trump in a statement in March, 2016 during the night Republican presidential debate said that he was softening his position due the accusation leveled against him. Trump said that he was still consistent in his earlier promise of eradicating the ever increasing H-1B abuse. He however insisted that he would end the use of H-1B first for every visa and immigration program and substitute it with a better venture of hiring American workers. Initially, the billionaire as well as the famous Republican presidential candidate was being accused of softening his position saying that he would be very liberal and lenient if probably elected to the office and post of the United States president. Trump antagonized the assertion by declaring unequivocally that he would always serve to the best interest of the masses and promised without hesitation that he would abolish the use of the H-1B and embark on a more viable venture which is replacing the hiring of American workers for the said H-1B use.

Trump in his response to a question which asked him whether he believed that engaging more skilled foreign workers to H-1B visas would reduce the number of workers in US, said that the country needed highly skilled manpower.

Despite all accusations and debates that ensued, Trump maintained that he would remain committed to eradicating the widespread of H-1B abuse and put to an end to such shocking and devastating practices like the one that occurred at Disney in Florida when Americans were coerced into training their foreign replacements.

Speaking on issues of unlawful immigration

Recently, Donald Trump made an urgent appeal to the working-class voters who had been gathered for the purpose of creating the new government. He advised them to ensure they go for election on February 9th 2016. He emphasized that the prerequisite for success in the election was their full participation in the election process. His speech marked the final event that took place in a campaign trail that took place in a town-hall meeting at Exeter.

The billionaire also added that his on-going hotel would be built fully very soon. He said this when he was addressing the audience in a tally at Portsmouth. He added that the hotel was being built for the purpose of transforming the old post office.

His transition into campaigning in small scale continued when his advisers announced another town hall in New Hampshire. He spoke on the issue of unlawful immigration, tagging himself the most uncompromising figure among all the aspirants. He also said, that immigrants would be allowed into the country but in a more legal and legitimate means.

Trump however, is one of the Republican presidential candidates who has used the immigration issue to propel voters. In regards to trade, Trump promised to restore the empty factories in New Hampshire. He blamed Obama and other Republican leaders for giving room for what he called the American economic decline. He then, promised social security and job creation for the masses.

Reaction to immigration issues in debate

Trump was present in a debate with seven other presidential candidates. At first, he was asked whether he was sympathetic to those agitating for a minimum wage of $15 per hour. Especially considering the fact that the tax plan gives a zero-income tax clause to citizens making $25 or less yearly. Trump responded positively, thereby receiving the applause of the audience. He added that the wages and tax had been too high and promised that they would not compete against the world. He said that the minimum wage would not be raised.

In another development, the immigration issue debate was raised and he promised to tighten the border to the extent that only legal individuals can have their way in. Trump got terrified when he was asked whether he would depot 50,000 immigrants. In his response "the immigrants must surely leave but can also come back more legally".

Trump was quiet for sometimes, when the issue of flat tax rate ensued in the debate, he didn't utter any word for 15 minutes but said later-on that they all have a different tax plan, and that he never agreed with some. He also said that each of them is better than the ones present now. This statement kept the audience in suspense due to its lack of clarity.

Disputably Trump's worst moment in the debate was when he was asked about his stand in the Trans-Pacific Trade Deal. He said that China could always come through the door just as they usually do.

Abortion

Argument with Rubio about abortion

In a Thursday night's debate in February 2016, Marco Rubio made a strong comeback rumbling the Presidential candidate Donald Trump, backed by a firm study of opposition. Rubio alleged Trump as a fraud, calling him a business person who supports illegal immigration. Rubio noosed Trump from all sides, slamming his ideology for foreign policy and determined Trump's plan to repeal Obamacare as visionless.

Above all, the Florida Senator served the best dish with all the spices Trump is known serve out himself. He jibed Trump that he would have been selling watches in Manhattan if had not his father gifted him the prosperous wealth of $200 million.

At the CNN debate, it was very clear that the competitors themselves Rubio and Sen. Ted Cruz had teamed up to take down Donald Trump (The biggest rival). Their strategy was crucial to win them Texas and Florida (home states) or their campaign will succumb to end. Resistant to the allegations the orotund personality Trump, most of the times remained unaffected. Trump performed a loyalty check for his supporters by pulling assertions on the sensitive issues like 'Planned Parenthood' and 'Israel' issue.

Trump also mentioned Planned Parenthood as a reason for cervical cancer and breast cancer calling himself pro-life and a critic of abortion. Trump played the Middle East card by mentioning his bond with Israel and cleared his stance on the dialogue between Israel and Palestine. Trump mentioned that he could play no role in the peace dialogue between Israel and vicinity countries. Baffling at this Rubio slammed the Palestinians for patronizing terrorists and working under black belief. It is believed that Trump can escape this policy positions only because of his stand for a new Republican Party. This promise was uttered during the confrontation of Trump's unpopularity among Latinos.

Pro-life stance of Donald Trump

Just after the decease of Supreme Court Just Antonin Scalia, Ted Cruz was in the headlines for an advertisement. This stimulant ad concerned was a topic of concern for Donald Trump who wants the ad to be removed.

The advertisement shows Trump as an untrustworthy candidate to appoint Scalia's successor as Trump was a strong supporter of abortion rights. The ad subjected as "Supreme Trust" is about Trump's interview, where the NBC host Tim Russert asked Trump about his opinion on the ban of partial-birth abortion. To which the then unsuccessful Presidential nominee, Trump, responded that he is pro-choice.

The advertisement by Cruz quite significantly questions Trump's stance using his previous statements. The narrator of the ad swiftly uses the statements of Trump's to point him as untrustworthy with a side notation of the interview being aired on 24th Oct 1994. Revoking the previous stand, Trump, in a June 2015 CNN interview shared his "pro-life" stance on the appointment of Supreme Court justices.

Trump has repeatedly mentioned in his interviews about his pro-life stance, one such instance is in an August 2015 'Meet the Press' interview, where Trump clarified about the previous interview that he was not a politician at the time and is being dragged for political vendetta. In the same interview, he mentions that abortion is a necessary and should be legal for victims of rape and incest or the mother under risk during delivery. A step further, Trump created an 'opinion column' calling himself 'pro-life'.

Trump also wrote that fund-raising of abortion providers is like demeaning people's self-respect at the least and disgrace good governance at the summit. Adding limitations to Cruz's new ad; it provides Russert's question on abortion but eliminates trump's response that he 'hates' abortion.

Prominent actions were taken before the 2016 election year and after that interview of 1999. The U.S Supreme Court stopped the "Partial Birth

Abortion Ban Act of 2003" which the congress members approved that specifically allowed to save the mother's life. Also, as of February 2016, according to the Institute of Guttmacher, 32 provinces enacted the ban on partial-birth abortions.

Psychological aspect of Trump's followers

People call him crazy, a narcissist, a New York liberal with a comb-over but Donald Trump is a persona who won't get off easily. The press ridiculed his lengthy speeches. Some even thought that Trump shall stay popular by his remark on Senator John McCain calling him "not a war-hero".

Baffling everyone, Trump's stars are much brighter in the race for Republican presidential nominations. Even the Republicans are bemused, calling Trump's believer insane but the psychologists have something logical to say. Interactions with psychologists and other intellectuals suggest a single reason for Trump's success. The experts mention that the unique ability of human's mind attracted to boasting and simple solutions for huge problems is the reason for this.

Trump beseeches using various sources, Trump's speech triggers the nostalgia so eminently, the fact that Trump was a reality star, his stand on the immigration policy are some of the few reasons psychologists count for Trump's large-scale following.

Trump's speeches vary from other representatives; he does not present scripted dialogues to witness audience's applause. He has his own charisma and style known as "word salad". Stanford's Jeffrey Pfeffer, psychologists calls Trump an effective orator and voters, the students who listen to politicians on the box just like in class. Pfeffer mentions narcissism as an important factor to win voters interests.

Pfeffer applauds Trumps dynamism, power and body language during his speech to which the voters relate and respond. He says energy is contagious. Psychologists have mentioned some specific qualities that human brains attract during trump's speech. "Seeking answers", the human brain seeks an answer for everything. We may not find correct answers but this dubiety is non-complacent. Hibbing of the Nebraska University admits this urgency as an important parameter to understand Trump's following.

Hibbing mentions that Trump is circulating the exact notion required by the people.

"We are gregarious"

Trump's move is the exact opposite of the Republican National Committee who called for impressing voters on the basis of their race. Trump appealed to those who are affected by immigrant's presence. This notion of providing a better option is deeply contrasting the common expectations. Experts believe this notion as the possible reason that majority finds convincing. Ultimately it is human nature. Trump lags by a huge margin in the recent polls.

To succeed the nomination race, Trump has to win even his non-supporters which are a tough task. Still the onus could be on his side as Trump is part and image of our continuous proneness. Hibbing argues that Human's nature is not final and can be overcome through discipline and practice.

Raising voice on Planned Parenting

Donald Trump raised his voice on Planned Parenthood, a non-profit organization for reproductive health, for the abortion option it offers in its healthcare plans. He insisted that they must stop offering abortion facility while adding that he couldn't recall ever donating to the organization. These concerns were expressed by Trump during 'Meet the Press' on NBC to the host of the show, Chuck Todd.

He voiced his dislike of the series of tapes that contained videos of discussions among the Planned Parenthood officials of the fetal tissue work of the organizations. Trump said it was terrible and that they talked about childbirth as if they were talking about making widgets or cars. He also added that it was inappropriate and that it should be stopped immediately.

The presidential candidate and billionaire admitted that he couldn't recall donating to the group, but it is possible since he donated money to many organizations in the past years. He also gave a detailed explanation about when he would agree that abortions are permissible. Incest, rape and if the mother is going to die during birth, were some exceptions he provided where abortions should be permitted. He also added that Ronald Regan and many Republicans have the same exceptions as he does.

Trump on women's issues

On 10th September 2015 Donald Trump, billionaire TV personality and presidential candidate talked to 'The View' about women's issues. After a clarification of his thoughts about immigration and Iran he moved on to talk about his popularity among Republican women voters.

When he was told to share a message for women, he said that he cherishes, respects women and would protect and take care of them. He then spoke of his commitment towards the healthcare of women. The host of the show took this opportunity to ask the presidential candidate about his thoughts on Planned Parenthood.

Trump replied saying that he hated abortion and the Planned Parenthood organization carries out a large number of abortions. Whoopi Goldberg gave a recommendation to Trump to get a bit more informed on issues of women and Behar explained the activities of the organization to Trump saying they only do abortions to 3% of the women who come to them and the rest of the 97% is related to women's health. She also said to Trump that he might want to extend the big heart he has for Syrians for women of the country as well.

The segment ended before Trump could respond to the host and the audience but the hosts promised to continue the conversation in a later segment of 'The View'.

Guns

Trump Vows to Restore Lost N. C Jobs in Fayetteville

Jaymie Baxley/Civitas Media Donald actually took hours cautioning the media for taking their pictures, fastened to the North Carolina for the rally that was hosted in Fayetteville in March 2016. Thousands of the supporters were thrown to disorder up to 15 times by those who display group feelings.

The aggressive billionaire has been proven to be at the fore front of the Republican delegate race. He has been promising too many things which no politician may actualize. The fans were in a happy mood as he shouted the names of the 14 primaries he won in the 20 states. He immediately left for the North Carolina, where the electorates would converge for the election.

He unveiled that he employed a lot of workers in the North Carolina which no Presidential candidate had ever done. Trump, in addition, had up to 53 percent of the votes casted at the election at the Robeson GOP convention. Trump added that he is the best Presidential candidate they had imagined. He said he is not an expert in politics but would run against those who had run for office their whole life.

Trump expressed frustration over the state of Washington. He further promised to take care of everything including veterans and all the things the troop requires. He also, promised the second amendment and unveiled that for the fact they have mental issues, they should therefor protect the second amendment.

After these he walked on the stage to the Alan Project shortly after 7pm and spent a lot of time dismissing them. He called the gathering to closure with a promise to revitalizing employment opportunities in North Carolina and promised them that their country would be a better place of living and that through his good leadership, the love of their President would be instilled in them.

Trump suggests use of guns in school grounds

The statements from Trump on a Saturday in October 2015 was the largest ever he made ever since he launched his campaign in June. He buttressed on his license to go about with gun in USA and for this rationale, he would never hesitate to reciprocate should any one tries to attack him.

Trump attributed mental issue to the cause of gun shooting in the US. His statement was very touching and wide. About nine people were shot dead and nine were injured in the process of shooting a few days back. It is not new anymore that Trump had always suggested the use of gun on school grounds.

An advocate of gun rights

'Trump supported the use of gun' evidenced in the paper he released last month. He added in the paper that the right of the people to use gun as was amended in the constitution was obvious and the right should by no means be violated.

He therefore, encouraged the use of gun and buttressed that the right of defense should not end at the driveway, but should also; involve the use of arms in the 50 States as to protect to a high extent, the right of human self-defense in the country.

In contrary, in July Trump also opted for a stop in the use of gun due to the shooting that triggered in Chattanooga, Tennessee which killed four Marines and a Sailor.

But after the mayhem Trump said that if he eventually became the President he would never expect to totally stop all public shootings, since there are some people in the society that could not be stopped.

He further stated that it is not correct in politics to unequivocally say this but the fact remained that there would be difficulties for the next million years and people would tremendously suffer.

Trump's decision changes on gun control

The businessman and billionaire Donald Trump has been parading himself as a truth-teller. But the determinant factor is the state of his past political career.

Come to think of it, it is evident that by using his past political detail as a criteria for his assessment, he has failed to be consistent. Most of the time Trump has tagged himself a free hearted man. But when guessed by the voters, his aggressiveness has made it difficult to summarize he is one.

As follows are the reasons evidencing that Trump has never been consistent at all;

In regards to health care, he used to welcome all sort of changes executed by Obamacare which has helped millions of Americans. Trump described himself as very lenient and receptive when it comes to health care, during an interview in 1991. In his book published in the year 2000,"The America We Deserve ", Trump suggested a single payer plan for USA which implies that the federal government should be the only provider of health insurance but most surprisingly, in his recent appearances he opted for Obamacare repeal evidencing his degree of inconsistency. In his book published in 2000, he fought against gun control but is recently supporting gun ownership.

At times he is inconsistent on his description of the political figures. He described Jeb Bush as a good man but has switched over to calling him a failure because he is competing with him. Also in 2015, he tagged Hillary Clinton, a terrific and hardworking woman but now refer to her as the worst Secretary right from the evolution of the country.

Right to use arms in second amendment

The Presidential head runner released a policy proposal that encompasses the importance of a second amendment as well as the right to use arms. The paper adopted the liberalization of gun use in the country.

According to the billionaire, the right of the people to hold gun cannot be violated which is clear in the second amendment of the constitution. This new gun proposal is in three focus; defending the rights of the legitimate gun users, enforcing book laws and fixing of spoilt mental health system.

He started by unveiling that he would prosecute criminals in Cities like Baltimore, Chicago and other uncontrollable ones. He expressed sadness on the release of drug dealers and promised that it would stop. He said that since security cannot be everywhere, the importance of legal gun use cannot be over-emphasized.

In the issue of broken mental health system, he opined that the murdering tragedy would have been prevented if more proactive measures were taken. More treatment programs should be embarked on because most people with mental issues are not violent but just need help, he said. Trump, proposed to putting into normalcy, the criminal background system rather than expanding it. He said that those who go through the background checks are the law abiding gun owners. The background checks is not effective because many States fail to keep criminal and health records, he said.

He concluded by saying that stopping the military from using firearms on the bases and at training centers remains absurd, since they train the military on how to use firearms and for this rationale, to keep them defenseless is ridiculous.

Best republican candidate with a gun

With the vow by the remaining candidates of the Republican Party to overturn the executive actions taken by President Obama on gun control, photographs of them carrying guns and rifles emerged. Donald Trump was one to publicly declare his love for hunting and his ownership of a gun. He also boasted that he owned a concealed-carry permit which is difficult to obtain in New York.

At an interview with Field and Stream, the presidential candidate mentioned that he has untied in his past years but it was discontinued due to his busy schedule. Trump also told that his two sons, Donald Jr. and Eric are also lifelong hunters and are proud members of the National Rifle Association (NRA) at the 2015 annual NRA meeting. Amidst the cheers and applause of his followers he expressed that nobody loves the Second Amendment as him and his supporters.

But when several photographs of his two sons with hunted wild animals resurfaced in 2011, Trump had a different idea about hunting. He said that he was not a believer of hunting and was surprised why his sons loved it. He was also against loosening the restrictions on gun ownership and mentioned it in his book, The America We Deserve published in 2000.

Regardless of the past, Trump now says he's a proud NRA member and supports to expand gun rights for law abiding citizens. He has also argued that it's the best way to stop the occurrence of mass shootings. In April, 2015 at the annual NRA meeting he exclaimed that he loves the NRA and loves the second amendment.

#MAKEAMERICAGREATAGAIN

Foreign Policy

Treating Israel better

Trump, the Republican President aspirant pledged that Israelites would no longer be treated as second class citizens if he was elected. Trump said this in his speech before the American Israel Public Affairs Committee.

Trump unequivocally unveiled that, Hillary Clinton and President Obama have failed to treat the Israelites well. He said in February that he would always play neutral in the peace dialogue between Israel and Palestinians but a few days back, in March 2016, promised to support them which is contrary to his initial alteration.

Like many Republicans, Trump struck Obama's recent deal with Israel's contenders, Iran in which the unreliable Middle East nation agreed to reduce her exchange of weapons for billions. He said that the first in his objective was to remove the non-beneficial deal with Iran, which he said to reduce the extent of his bad deal. Trump argued that Iran had been a threat across the Middle East by supplying weapons to terrorists like Hezbollah which he promised to abolish. He promised to whole put a stop to Iran's global terror network.

He also, made a promise of moving the U. S embassy from Two Aviv to Jerusalem. Trump also said, he would move the U.S. embassy from Tel Aviv to Jerusalem, the eternal capital of the Jewish. He also promised consistency in his promise to supporting the Jewish State coupled with the partnership between the United States and Israel. Trump made many promises aimed at getting their votes. Even at the presence of many antagonists, he remained consistent in his manifesto, that he would be the best President ever, if elected.

Trump Unveiled That He Wasn't Pandering About Israel

Trump, the Republican Presidential aspirant in his speech in March 2016, spoke in favor of Israel and struck against Iran and the United Nations. Trump vividly told those in presence at the conference that Iran was a big problem to the Middle East. He however, denounced the nuclear deal.

According to him the most important thing in the deal was that they should keep to the terms of the deal by merely running out the clock. He stated clearly that he wasn't present at that night to tempt Israel but to let them know what he would accomplish. He promised them that he would equate their citizenship with other citizens of the country and further put that all forms of segregation and impartiality against them would be totally abolished.

Trump also campaigned against the United Nations with the view that the international body was malfunctioning. He opined that the United Nations was never friendly to democracy. He promised to disapprove any United Nations' attempt to impose any order on Israel. He criticized the treating of Israel as second class citizens. Trump tried to avoid his initial statements that U.S should remain silent about the peace dialogue between Israel and Palestinians. He said that for the fact that the United Nations was not free to democracy which is the pillar of their country amendments would be made in that direct if elected.

Trump alleged that President Barack Obama was the worst thing to happen to Israel as he had always supported the unfair treatment against Israel. He spoke to reporters earlier that he was in Washington to address fellow Republicans.

Trump, despite many criticisms he encountered, maintained that he would do the best ever for Israel unlike the past government of President Barack Obama.

Discussion about Israel between Trump, Cruz and Rubio

A heated discussion occurred between the billionaire presidential candidate Donald Trump and the US state senators Marco Rubio and Ted Cruz at the big GOP debate in February 2016. The topic of the discussion was Israel and making peace efforts with Palestinians. All 3 politicians tried to prove that they were the ones who supported Israel most.

Trump expressed that there is nothing he would do rather than bringing peace to Israel and its neighboring countries. He admitted that he may not achieve success in bringing peace to the situation but also said that being pro-Israel there is no use of demeaning its neighbors as support. Ted Cruz made accusation to Trump as being similar to Hilary Clinton on this matter saying that both of them wants to be neutral.

Rubio on the other hand said that Trump's stance on the matter is actually anti-Israel though he may not realize it. He said that you can't be an honest broker in this dispute as Palestinian Authorities have neglected several peace attempts made by Israel. Marco Rubio took this an opportunity to say that the US needs someone like him who would stand on Israel's side.

Trump slammed Rubio by saying he's not a negotiator and brought up a previous argument between Rubio and a former candidate Chris Christie. Even though Rubio exclaimed that Palestinians are not a real estate deal, Trump stood firm in his stance.

Trump sends sparks flying in Worcester

Trump, the Republican presidential candidate addressed a question given to him in Worcester by his supporters. In response to a question about United States' response to ISIS, Trump described that he would increase the frequency of the ISIS bombing to the degree that no one can ever believe it. The other questions he was asked encompassed the foreign policy issue, Syrian refugee crisis and his famous brash attitude. In his response to the Syrian issue he declared his intention of the US troops invading Syria and especially ensuring that other countries fights ISIS. He also supported Gov. Charlie Baker who opined that he wouldn't like to see Syrian refugees in his state unless with a proper federal plan. Trump said that if elected, he would totally stop refugees from entering into the country.

Trump was also asked about his stand on the German Jewish refugees in Jan. the 1930's. His response was that he would have allowed them into the country since they weren't going to knock down the World Trade Center.

He was also asked by a reporter about his initial statement of shutting down mosques; they asked him whether he would also do same to churches, temples and synagogues .He said he wouldn't, since he had not seen any mayhem emanating from those religious groups. Another question that arose was whether the Muslims would vote for him having said that the Mosques would be shut down. He said they would probably vote for him. One reporter wondered if he had the right temperament, he responded yes since what they needed in America was strong temperament.

Trump criticized his opponents by viewing them as politicians who only talk but no action to justify their statement. He pinpointed the differences between him and them, for instance funding of his campaign as well as his stance against Super-PACs.

Trump Thinks President Barack Obama Hates Israel

Donald Trump, the Republican presidential candidate has alleged that President Barack Obama detests Israel. In his speech in a rally at Reno, Nevada, a day following the third Republican debate Trump unveiled that many friends never knew what transpired with the US support of Israel in light of the Iran's nuclear deal. Trump unveiled that the Israelis believes that

President Barack Obama actually detests them extremely. The billionaire supported and said he suggest so too.

The billionaire and Republican presidential candidate said that the Iran's deal was very bad for Israel and had posed a lot of trouble and setback since the country reached the agreement. The billionaire expressed optimism, if elected. He was so optimistic that he would surely deliver and save Israel as well as take the entire country to another higher level. The above comment was made by him when the audience commenced shouting, "what about Israel? ". Trump unequivocally said that he would be the only savior to Israel. He said one of his agenda would be to ensure that Israel was saved as he had come to emancipate them. He enjoined all the Israelites to ensure they cast their votes for him as this would be the only determinant factor for enslaving them.

#MAKEAMERICAGREATAGAIN

Taxes

Trump on tax returns

Donald Trump, the controversial presidential candidate in US had planned to welcome New Yorker Michael into the presidential contest, if he eventually decide to run. The billionaire said this on NBC's "meet the press". He unequivocally unveiled that he would like to see Michael Bloomberg contest with him. He however, expressed optimism to his supporters that he is capable enough of challenging Bloomberg, should he eventually decide to compete with him.

Trump also responded to the appeal made to all candidates to release their tax returns before early election commences. He said that his team was working on it and added that since he had a high tax returns and everything had been approved, they would surely settle it. But when eventually he was pressed to state the particular date he would deliver the tax documents, he spoke favorably in defense of himself and said he didn't know since it is not a normal tax return. Trump however, expressed regret of not understanding what his tax payment was used for.

Trump further attacked Ted Cruz, his rival, by putting forward that Ted was a guy who nobody likes and further added that even though he worked with the Republican senators, no one had endorsed him. Finally, in response to a criticism against him that a new conservative should not pilot the affairs of the conservative movement, he used Ronald Reagan as an instance who was a liberal democrat, who later became a new conservative and later also became a good president.

Tax payment of high income earners

Trump answered vehemently when he was accused of proposing higher taxes, national health care and the Wall Street bailout. He responded no, and tagged himself a liberal. Trump posited that in many cases he identified himself as a democrat.

In regards to tax, Trump said that there were high income earners in the country who pay little or no tax. He however posited that this act was wrong. Trump also said that the rate of tax paid in the country was not enough and so suggested the payment of additional tax. In a recent interview Trump refused to accept flat rate tax and said that he believed that people who their income increased could pay a higher percentage. He however declared that the government must be run with money and so a reasonable tax payment is imperative. Trump also called for a government run healthcare and said that this would be made possible only with an increase in tax rate.

Trump added that he wants to cancel Obamacare and substitute it with, what according to him is called Donaldcare. He also promised to build the U.S product by blowing off the tax on imported goods ranging from 25 to 30 percent precisely. He promised that Americans should be ready to buy things more costly since the producer passes tax burden to the consumers.

Trump considers himself the only noble and brave man who could make things happen. He thinks the president can always give orders every time in the home, government, businesses and neighborhood. He did not understand clearly the constitution's power of limiting the power of strongmen like him.

Donald Trump's Socialist Idea

It is astounding that the Republican presidential aspirant, Donald Trump had in the past approved a lenient and liberal economic ideas. It is however surprising that Trump had supported the imposition of a high tax on the super-rich. In November, 1999, the billionaire supported a 14.25 percent tax on the total wealth of all individuals and corporate bodies with a net worth of $10 million or above.

Trump's plan critically makes assessment of the individual's wealth less the value of the principal residence. This strategy would coerce people into making their assets liquid and sell stocks as well as real estate investment in order to be able to pay taxes. He posited that the strategy would increase the nation's income by $5.7 trillion which would help reduce national debt. Trump further buttressed that one percent of the American population would be affected by his plan while 99 percent would experience a severe reduction. Trump's adoption of these strategies had been to reduce inequality among the citizens and hence create a balance in the economy. Trump's assumption gave the government more power to influencing the activities of the private sector which America as a country does not advocate.

Person's like Dean Baker applauded Trump's proposition for a net worth tax but pondered whether it could be enforced since America does not allow government interference. Trump had changed his tune since then.

Trump would bring down the high tax on the income taxes of the rich coupled with reducing the top additional rate from 40 percent to 25 percent which is the very same rate he criticized.

#MAKEAMERICAGREATAGAIN

Healthcare

Six years of affordable care act

Six years from today, an act of Affordable care also known as 'Obama Care' was signed by the President of USA Barack Obama. The whole event was commemorated at PSE&G Children's Specialized Hospital in the presence of ministers and barristers at New Brunswick.

Here is what some party members commented regarding the celebration. Jackie Cornell Bechelli, Regional Director for Department of Health and Human Services, mentioned that approx. a quarter million Americans have been covered under Obamacare and ten millions are still to be covered. He also appreciated the initiative by lauding the expansion of Medicaid with 500,000 people of New Jersey and 288,000 new consumers being covered. The department also claimed that the Obamacare Health plan costs only $75/month after including all the concessions.

Herb Conaway, chairman of Assembly Health Committee and a Democrat compared that after the Affordable Care Act and treating the patients, suddenly with a health cover, he can now provide a large number of medicines for chemotherapy, which wasn't available to him before the Act.

The real allegations were made by Mr. Donald Trump who denounced the Act. Donald Trump also annunciated to repeal the Obamacare and change it with something which he mentions to be superior, 'if' he wins the White House in the upcoming elections.

Responding to Trumps statement, Joe Vitale, Chairman of Senate Health Committee and a Democrat, calls the statement insane and thoughtless. He also questioned Trump and the Republicans if they are going to revoke Obamacare by hauling it away from the patients in the middle of their chemotherapy and leave them to pay those ransoms on their own.

Cornell Bechelli again excerpted that the number of people who have opted the insurance is in millions and they cannot be wrong.

As the court has stayed the Act two times, the Supporters were sure about Supreme Court's decision, regardless of any party winning the White House race.

Donald Trump's -"Trumpcare"

In March, 2016 Donald Trump unveiled his much-awaited manifesto describing the plan to improve the 'Affordable Care Act'.

Trump was caught on record, stating Obamacare as a financial trouble for Americans. Trump also called Obama the most schismatic and partial President ever. According to Trump the prevalent health plan is a complete failure passed by biased ministers of the House that have resulted in higher costs and minimum choices. Trump mentions that his proposals are ought to be considered by the congress on the very first day of Trump's government to provide financial freedom to the Americans.

Trump believes that the Medicaid needs to be a block-grant program and the Americans deserve to opt for health cover across the state lines. In his manifesto, he promises to offer a safer, cheap and stable medicine by allowing the free market to drug suppliers. Trump's plan says that Americans deserve a courageous government who steps away from partiality and work for the people.

The front runner of the Presidential race also said that his denotations will definitely improve the health care expenses for every citizen of America. Trump also indicated that he is ready for suggestions and will consider them if the reforms result in the reduction of expenses. The proposal also offered a promise to eliminate any confusion and create an economically secure environment for the citizens. Trump also emphasized on the elimination of fraudulent policies, imposing immigration laws and relieving the financial pressure of every citizen, ultimately leading to reduced healthcare charges and burden.

Trump says Republicans will let people to die

The Telephonic interview of Donald Trump with Sean Hannity highlights Trump's bold stance on some Republicans. Trump calling some Republicans callous, expressed that those people are so insensitive that they would allow a person to die even outside the treatment center or a hospital.

The conversation between Trump and Hannity was regarding the ongoing issues and Trump's stance of health care. On ABC's show 'This Week' Trump did not hesitate to call Ted Cruz heartless for bashing Trump only on health care issue rather Trump just wants to 'Make America Great Again'.

He also said that there are people who deserve care and proper attention; they cannot be left to succumb on the streets. Clarifying his stance on Republicans, he mentioned that the party people comprehend this very much and are sensitive.

However, he did not change his statement about some Republicans who can intentionally leave some people to death without any regret. Manifesting that Trump agreed to loses his share of vote for this reason.

#MAKEAMERICAGREATAGAIN

Economy

Donald Trump in Kasich's Ground

In March 2016, Donald Trump with a motive to end Ohio's Governor John Kasich's campaign tried to project Kasich as a job killer. In order to strengthen his support, Trump was at a badly affected steel country near Youngstown where most of the mills are producing rust these days. In search of an approachable audience in Ohio, Trump promised to bring back the jobs that are being contracted to foreign suppliers.

The businessman shouting from an airplane hangar called Ohio an integrated part of America that could make it great again meanwhile discrediting Kasich. This rally of Trump's was unusual from others as there was no protest. One reason was the bridging of guests and removing them from a nearby shopping mall, leaving the rebels stranded once they are identified.

Ignoring Kasich before, Trump was inexorable against him this time. In his speech Trump pronounced Kasich an over-rated governor. Showing the stats of Ohio's falling economy Trump reminded for the urgency of oil in the state.

Kasich is a huge competitor to Trump and polls are showing the same. Although Kasich has not won a single state but could spoil Trumps path if he wins Ohio. The message has been flown very well by his supporters during recent rallies that voting Kasich is actually abandoning Trump.

Winning Ohio and enough representatives shall strengthen Trump's nomination from the Republican. It would be mighty if he loses Ohio but could manage to reach the required 1237 representatives. A Kasich win ensures the Republican to choose zero nominees. Trump trying his best to rectify this, accommodated the voters without any conditions in the Mahoning Valley. Trump also promised to bring the economy on track.

Trump paraphrased air-conditioning manufacturers to show his will to pull the entire industries on track. He promised to coerce the working man by calling himself not very presidential. In the very speech he also talked about the Ford factory away from the airport of Cleveland and bringing jobs to the country. Anticipating an economically shattering trade war, Trump assured a 35% excise on goods being imported.

Meanwhile, he proposed free trade agreements as the main cause of depression. Trump also blamed Mexico, China, India and Vietnam from where most of the immigrants fly to the country as a major reason for American youth's unemployment.

Trump concluded the event by bashing Kasich. He took enough of his closing time to satisfy Kasich with a second position in the race. He even reminded the voters of Kasich's NAFTA deal and asked them to reject him. He also warned about the recent Pacific deal yet to be signed by Kasich that could lead to shutting down of automobile enterprises. Beyond the usual rant that signifies Trump rallies, the presenter was unstoppable against Kasich. A Kasich win is the last threat to Trump's nomination.

Trump wants to Hire American first

Donald Trump, the self-acclaimed Presidential candidate is back with his recently published immigration plan. The plan concatenates the ideas and thoughts of the lower assembly's strongest H-1 B opponents. The plan emphasizes to make it overpriced or difficult to replace native workers with foreign labor.

In no time, Senator Jeff Sessions (R-Ala), the chair of the assembly's Immigration Subcommittee applauded the immigration plan and dedicated Trump's overall policy proposal as an exact plan for America. Trump's proposal highlights an increment in the existing honorarium resulting in high priced H-1 B labor. Although Trump has not pronounced an exact action plan for existing wage levels, some supporters have opposed the elimination of low prevailing-wage levels.

Trump mentions in his plan that the hike in the fees paid to H-1 Bs will influence the companies to replace the foreign pool with native workers. Trump also wants to make it compulsory to hire local Americans first. He also writes about the urgency of hiring domestic personnel to reduce the unemployment circle.

He also calls his proposal a measure to balance the Hispanic and Black labor ratio in Silicon Valley, who has become prey because of the present H-1 B policy.

Vermont Senator Bernie Sanders an independent candidate labels the H-1 B program as a 'supply of employment' overseas. Trump who wants the Republic nomination is very close to Sanders regarding the H-1B criticism. While some have called Trump's proposal exactly aligned to the U.S ideology including Sen. Chuck Grassley (R-Iowa), the chair of the Judiciary Committee and Sen. Dick Durbin.

It can be noticed that Trump's views on H-1 B are linked with the narration and belief of two scholars, Ron Hira, an associate professor of public policy at Howards University and Hal Salzman, professor of planning and public policy at Rutgers University. In last election campaigns, the alleged visa policy had been invisible. By making it a major part of his immigration platform, Trump playing it wittily has raised the problem's profile and allowed others to connect with it. That could ultimately instigate a higher level debate regarding the visa policy.

Tariff on foreign goods

The four Republican presidential candidates attended the 12th debate of the party hosted by CNN at the University of Miami. Marco Rubio, Ted

Cruz and Donald Trump answered and debated on several questions related to economy, crime, safety etc. of the United States.

When asked about visas for highly skilled workers, Donald Trump said that as a businessmen, he uses it because that is what he has to do. But at the same time he added that it's unfair for the workers and it should be ended.

The reason for holding Trump's news conference at Mar-a-Lago, a private club owned by him was also revealed during the debate when Trump declared that Ben Carson, a retired neurosurgeon will be endorsing him.

Ted Cruz and Donald Trump argued over the threat of imposing 45% tariff on foreign goods, by Trump. When Trump said it's a threat that will be a tax only in foreign countries like China, an enraged Cruz argued saying it will be the working citizens in the US that will have to pay this tax and not the Chinese.

But Trump argued back explaining that he would build the necessary plants and factories in the US without importing goods and that it would also create more jobs for the Americans as well.

After talking about Trump's ideas on Muslims and the safety of the country, the debate ended with Cruz and Trump declaring who has the more possibility of gaining the nomination.

Civil Liberties

Donald Trump wants a close monitoring of certain mosques

Trump requested to know who the people coming from the Trojan horse were.

Trump, in November 2015 had been antagonized for having made a controversial statement of tracking the Muslims' database. The story had dominated everywhere in the country. Having had the rumor from his antagonists, Trump responded and told them he needed a surveillance of some mosques. He asked the crowd whether they were ready for it. He however, made it clear that he would want a close monitoring of certain Mosques. Trump said this because of the alleged mayhem to the Muslims. For this reason he had always insisted and opted for a more careful look on the various Mosques in the country.

"These people that are coming in the Trojan horse. I want to know who the hell they are," said Trump. This week Trump has been criticized for his controversial comments about creating a database to track Muslims. This message made a tremendous value to the ideas of his supporter, and they hence agreed with his security plan due to the recent Paris attacks.

The rally was also disturbed by those who display group feelings. One of them was caught by Trump and he vehemently asked him out. He later directed the police to throw him out as a result of his disturbance. But it is worthy of note that nobody was apprehended or arrested by his security despite the degree of disruption protesters unleashed.

Trump and others debates on personal property issues

Trump, the GOP front runner, spoke in February 2016, in Beaufort, S.C. The State intends carrying out its Republican presidential primary the following weekend.

A debate as to whether property owners should be coerced into giving out their public good for public use ensued. Some people were extremely concerned about it. For instance, Jackie Bartlet said she had recently seen surveyors along her property area and expressed disappointment over it.

One of the debaters said it was abnormal to forcefully take someone's property. According to him, the property owners should sell their properties by willingness and not under coercion.

Trump, at the second time the debate was carried over during the Republican debate stage, was on the defensive side of the issue. He said he had not any passion on the eminent domain and however, added that the eminent domain was needed strongly. The issue was also discussed in South Carolina Legislature. In this week, the Senators made an enactment that could ban the Palmetto pipeline developers from spoiling private lands emanating from the use of eminent domain. This very debate had been in hot state in South Carolina, said by one of the bills' sponsor.

Trump's stand on the issue was precise. He only spoke in defense of the issue for reasons best known to him. However, most debaters viewed that it was not good for people to snatch away, the property that belongs to people forcefully. They however said that, property owners should give out their properties by willingness.

Gay YouTube Personality 'Comes Out' In Support Of Donald Trump

Donald Trump, the GOP front-runner had for long supported equal right before Hillary Clinton proposed gay marriage, said Kittleson. In this article, we shall re-visit and have a holistic view of this issue. YouTube personality, Kyle Kittleson has religiously pledged his support for Donald Trump, the Republican presidential candidate. He therefore expressed vividly, that he would vote for the business man, Donald Trump.

It is evident that Kittleson, being a marine mammal trainer at seaWorld Orlando may eventually support Trump financially in his present presidential campaign. However, long before Hillary Clinton supported the concept of gay marriage, the present GOP front-runner had already proposed equal right for each and every individual in the country. This was altered by Kittleson in a clip. He further made reference with the 2000 interview to Trump which he advocated the support for workplace discrimination protection coupled with a strong law which gives equal legal protection to gay people and the married people. According to him, married and gay should have equal marriage right, since it does not in any way violate the law of the land.

However, the fact that Trump supported equal right and protection for both gay and married people cannot be over-emphasized or disputed, said Kittleson. According to him, Trump understands the meaning of human right and does not hesitate to keep it for the masses. Therefore, it will not be mistake tagging Trump, a human right advocate, due to his tremendous and incomparable support for human right.

Crime and Safety

Police officers are mistreated

The final GOP debate between the Republican Presidential candidates was held in February 2016. Participants of the debate included Jeb Bush, John Kasich and Chris Christie Governors of Florida, Ohio and New Jersey respectively and the candidates, Ted Cruz, Donald Trump and Marco Rubio.

After debating about many subjects like same sex marriage, abortion, terrorism and expressing each other's ideas, Trump reiterated his statement about Police officers. He said they are being mistreated despite the wonderful job they do. Even after keeping law and order intact, police officers are afraid of their job because of being mistreated, said Trump. Kasich weighed in to this offering a task force created by him to make improvements in the police by reducing the tension between them and minor communities.

Again after several other topics, Trump was asked what it would take to initiate military action towards North Korea. He responded saying that we have an incompetent current president who has no idea about what he is doing. And that president Barrack Obama is driving the country to hell with the actions he take towards crime and safety.

UMass police union disavows parent union's endorsement of Donald Trump

The endorsement of Republican Presidential candidate and billionaire business owner Donald Trump by their parent's union has been disavowed by the University of Massachusetts Amherst Police union. The reason was expressed saying that this endorsement does not display the views of the union membership.

Trump was endorsed by the New England Police Benevolent Association which has over 100 police departments in the region. The support for Trump is partly based on his statement about executing people convicted of murdering police officers, said Jerry Flynn, the Vice President of NEPBA. But the president of NEPBA Local 190 declared that he would not support Trump as it is not a part of the membership of their department to endorse a candidate, let alone a controversial one.

Trump in the meantime mentioned at the candidate forum in Portsmouth, New Hampshire that he would never let down the Police and law enforcement.

There were several parties against this decision including the Durham, New Hampshire police department and the Portsmouth Police Department. Westfield city councilor-elect Steve Dondley who owns the web development company that hosts the NEPBA's website also declared that he will discontinue business with the union due to this endorsement. Flynn responded saying that they had already decoded to halt the hosting before the endorsement and planned to hire a different web company.

Death penalty for killing police officers

Despite the conflicts in the constitution, Donald Trump reiterated his statement to give death penalty for people who murder cops. He further expressed his liking towards police officers and gratitude for their services to ABC news in December 2015. He also said that Police officers have been huge supporters of him and he wants to charge anyone who kills a cop with the death penalty.

When asked how he's going to accomplish it, Trump said he would work with states and do it in a federal basis if possible. This issue was raised by Trump previously when he made the controversial proposal to ban Muslim Americans coming to the country.

He further said that if he win he would sign a statement that would go beyond America that for anybody committing the crime of killing a male or female police officer will definitely be charged with the penalty of death.

Legal experts like Professor Deborah Denno, Forham University School of Law in New questioned the possibility of doing this saying that there had been only 37 Federal executions from the 1927. A law professor from the Columbia University, New York said that it is clearly mentioned by the Supreme Court that mandatory death penalty is problematic. He also said having a focused look at the individual and the committed crime is the whole point of the 8th amendment.

#MAKEAMERICAGREATAGAIN

Environment

The Chinese invention of the false climate change was fake

Donald, in response to one of his rival which tried to determine his stand on the climate change, said that the climate change as was invented by the Chinese was fake and useless. He said this on January 24 on NBC's meet the press. In Nov. 6, 2012, Trump tweeted also, that the Chinese invented the concept of global warming for the purpose of making the U.S manufacturing companies, non-competitive. Trump went further to telling Fox and friends, that, the climate change was a very costly form of tax, which he jokingly said that, it was done to the benefit of China since because, they have nothing to do to help the climate change. They constitute negative externalities and cared less, he said.

Trump had said also, said that his 2012 tweet was a lighter mood and had however, used the word "hoax" time without number, to describing climate change but has never placed blames on China. He told the crowd in Dec. 30, 2015, that the global warming was only a money making industry. Trump wondered in January 25, 2014, why his country was still spending money on global warming and added that it is an expensive hoax. He further unveiled that, he was tired of hearing the nonsense "global warming ".Also, in September, 24, 2015, Trump said he didn't believe in climate change. The above evidence has shown that he has not considered the said climate change a profitable venture due to its hoax nature and large disadvantages as he depicted. He further added that the global warming was done for the benefit of China which does not care at all or do anything in return.

Donald trump's opinion on climate change

The Republican Candidate for presidential election has released his opinion on climate change and his opinion is attributably, not in favor of it. Trump, told radio talk show, that unless somebody proved to him, he would always believe, there is weather and there is Change also. Trump however posited that the olden people in the 1920s thought the earth was cooling and now another perspective about the existence of global warming has ensued portraying that such scientific discoveries was typically nonsense, fake and hoax. Trump totally rejected the assertion, that there was global warming on earth and had therefore advocated the initial believe of the past people, that the earth was cooling.

Trump however blamed the government for attempting to bring solution to a problem that does not and had never existed on earth. Trump argued that placing more emphasis in global warming was useless since the weather moves up and down. He said the weather could rise or come down and so does not remain constant. He added that he actually believes on weather and its change. According to him, its changes was dependent on years and centuries. He further alleged President Obama as one of the problems, the world was having today due to his staunch believe in unrealistic things. The concept of global warming was created by the Chinese in order to reduce the competitive ability of the U.S manufacturing. He however, suggested that better issues and ventures should be embarked on rather than, engage in irrelevant things that would not yield any benefit.

Trump will kill our economy, climate and democracy

In a recent Trump's interview, Trump was told by the Pope that he was harmful and toxic. Those presence was silent trying to listen to what would be the response of the capitalist. Trump eventually, dodged the question and threatened the Pope that the ISIS would hunt him and take over his place of residence. That, he said to the Pope's face. He further said that he wanted to scare the Pope and further, urged him, to pray for the proper working of capitalism. He further exclaimed that, capitalism was not working very well in U.S due to government's regulation of industries and further dismissed the issue by positing that he is not of the believe that the Pope antagonizes capitalism. The Pope seemed against everything the Donald proposes. For instance, the Pope unequivocally, told Trump, that His GOP-style capitalism had continued to destroy the world by creating inequality coupled with other pitfalls that it encompasses.

Trump also, pinpointed that he was not a believer of the global warming but believed in weather timely changes. He said, that the global warming was very expensive and hoax and was created by the Chinese to reduce the competitive ability of the U.S manufacturing.

Trump has been known as an extreme capitalist who severely believes in the workings of capitalism and advocates profit, net worth earnings. He believes that government should not have an active participation in the economy as to enable the free flow of economic activities and of GDP in the country.

Trump further warns Obama that EPA was an impediment to jobs and growth and added that jobs would keep reducing until the price of oil comes down again. He however, criticized Obama for pissing billions of Money away on green energy which later failed.

Education

Things to know about trump

The following point critically explains the attributes and behavior of the GOP Republican front-runner;

Trump is actually not a type of person that could be bribed easily. It is evidence from the attestation of persons like Hugh Joyce. He is not a person that can be bought which makes him consistent in his statements, as he does not make a sudden change in whatever he had already said.

Many people are extremely surprised, especially the Republican establishment people over Trump's victory of the South Carolina primary competition in which he was able to capture all the 50 state delegates. The victory also compounded when he also captured 46 percent of the vote.

The business man owns about 500 businesses with an incomparably average worth. This is an evidence of his industriousness, business mindedness and competence. Many consumers are very interested in his products not minding the price since they portray that his goods is always up-to standard and superior.

Moreover, most campaign rally utilizes funds generally contributed or borrowed but the GOP front-runner, had however, been funding his campaign with his personal money which could be attributed to his wealth capability. It's just only a little fraction of the campaign fund that emanated from donors.

One other good attribute of Trump is the slashing of the corporate income tax from its initial 30% to 15%. This has been very interesting to businesses and corporate bodies. This means that price of the finished goods of such businesses will be comparably low and the value added tax would also be low due to the low business tax. The rationale for the tax cut according to him was business enlargement. Trump also, promised to lower the personal income tax as to increase disposable income. It is true also, that this policy would increase national debt.

Trump addresses thousands of people from behind a podium

Trump, in February 2016, engaged in retail politics. He held a microphone and addressed the audience in attendance. He spoke for about 2 minutes before he delved into the question and answer segment.

The first question they threw on him was what he would do to ensure that the national service opportunities developed. He responded that the issue was going to be looked at very seriously. He also criticized President Obama for taken the issue not important and essential. Another question thrown to him was, since he just recently gave birth to a daughter, whether she would be safe and also receive equal pay with them. Trump responded, she would be safe. Trump, also promised to assist the colleges financially if elected.

Trump, in his response to a 13 year old boy who asked him about his planned contributions to the national debt, said, he was going to make the country powerful and strong. He however advice the boy not to worry and go to school, since it is a prerequisite for success.

He also received another question about the possibility of telling the Syrian migrants to their face, that they were not going to school in the country. He responded precisely and said he could be bold to say it. He however promised to tell it to their face without any hesitation.

Trump, despite the fact that it was the final day before the primaries criticized some of his Republican opponents. For instance, he told Bush that he was like a child who is not in any way smart. People however, said that they have made up their minds already about who to vote for.

Trump shuts down US public schools

The Republican presidential candidate, Donald Trump has released a video which for the second time unveils his pledge to putting an end to common core and the US public schools which according to him was very bad and nothing to write home about. The video declared him an indefatigable believer in education. He however, advised that education should be at a local level. According to him, the chains of command in Washington should not be determining how a child's education would be managed. He therefore attributed bureaucratic procedures, a setback to schools and considered it a drawback to the educational quality of the US nation.

In another development Trump makes a precise but severe attack on the state and quality of the schools resident in US. He however, added that the 28 rating they had in the world as regards to school quality was very appalling. He expressed that they spend huge amount per pupil more than any other country in the world but yet no tangible result was gained. He further added that the 28th ranking by the Organization for Economic Cooperation and Development was very bad for them. Some criticisms were made against him. For instance, many countries like Austria, Switzerland and others even pay more than them. His alleged Washington bureaucracy that according to him, had influenced schools seems unrealistic, since many schools were not built by the federal government but other bodies. Finally, Trump characterizes himself the best candidate for the presidential election as against his opponents.

Budget and Spending

Donald Trump Abrades House Republicans over Budget deal

In case anyone does need some more exhibits for the American people persevering by virtue of their own organization, looks not more than the money related support deal proclaimed by Speaker Ryan, said Trump.

Mr. Trump joined that as an aftereffect of the supporting strategy, Americans ought to less budgetary adaptability, and adapt higher inadequacies, more colossal duty, and more corporate welfare. By what types of the philosophies would they be able to go up against their constituents when they continue upsetting our young people and the grandchildren with obligations they will never have the capacity to repay? Our board is falling flatus, so we ought to make a move.

Typically the most fundamental astounding interest are generally not being served by our association are the American individuals. Becoming frustrated he also said that we require a president who can lead the fight to hold Congress and the straggling leftovers of the organization dependable so that people can have a reliable governance.

Who knows how appalling things will be the time when the gang with affiliation comes in and necessities to get the pieces?" "It is time we constrained spending arrangement discipline by holding the line on spending, discarding waste, deception and abuse, and by handling our commitment," he said.

The Republican presidential verbal confrontation

At a night in December 2015, at the Republican presidential verbal confrontation, Ben Carson conveyed an opening articulation about the void of devastation. Marco Rubio, who talked about "the personality of America in the 21st century," was likewise at the secondary school level. Ted Cruz and John Kasich were at center school perception levels.

This was no abnormality. Some saw Trump's particularly mundane exposition right on time in the battle, yet it has turned out to be much more professional. This would seem to affirm surveying that shows Trump draws quite a bit of his backing from less-instructed Americans; "I adore the ineffectively taught," he said after his Nevada triumph.

This doesn't imply that all Trump supporters are moronic. Be that as it may, he is conveying intentionally, without a doubt at a considerably simpler level than any other competitor in either party. "He says five things," Rubio insulted night of Holy Thursday. "Everybody's imbecilic, he's going to make America awesome once more, we're going to win, win, win, his triumph in the surveys.

In any case, on some primal level, it works. Americans, particularly the people who are enraged and eager, as Trump's fans are wishing to be educated that they will be OK, that there are fundamental answers.

There is an obvious draw in Trump's life-changing announcement on the Middle East. "The considered absence of inclination is based upon the left getting to be tied up with this moral relativism that is much of the time contributed the media." This is suggested for forming lingo, however, associated with fight addresses and verbal meetings, it gives an unforgiving sentiment the relative levels of hopefuls' discussion.

In locations the night of the South Carolina fundamental, Rubio at an eighth-grade level and Trump at a fifth-grade level. In talks after Nevada social affairs, Cruz and Democrat Bernie Sanders were at a ninth-grade level, Hillary Clinton was at seventh grade.

Donald Trump on spending

Donald Trump showed up on MSNBC in a restrictive town corridor in Charleston, S.C., trying to counter-program Ted Cruz, his central opponent for the Republican assignment who was talking in the meantime on CNN." he proceeded with "It's an exceptionally miserable thing and kept on pounding at Cruz for his battle's activities in Iowa. Trump's town lobby, facilitated by Joe Scarborough and Mika Brzezinski, secured a scope of subjects.

When it came to name the applicant Brzezinski later tested Trump, requesting that he distinguish the competitor in light of the accompanying depiction: a presidential cheerful who is self-subsidizing his crusade, underpins social insurance for all and rails against Wall Street.

Scarborough caught up by inquiring as to whether he would utilize District of Columbia versus Heller as a litmus test for Supreme Court nominees.

They will be less in cost and they will be better," Trump said all Americans would have entry to human services, as they should under the Affordable Care Act, Trump said that he would work out an arrangement with healing facilities and groups. In light of a few inquiries fixating on outside approach and the war in Iraq, he said that he was representative, not a government official.

To distinguish three individuals he would counsel with however said he wanted to name an outside arrangement group in a week, repeated lines from his stump discourse about how current monetary strategies make it outlandish for the United States to contend with so much nations as China, Japan and Mexico.

He will give it a serious shot. That is the hardest arrangement on the planet to make, he said. It needs to last to finish off the town lobby, somebody in the group of onlookers asked Trump for what valid reason he was running for the race, then he addressed that he could have been spotted someone else, however he is here.

National Security

Nuclear weapon usage

At an interview with the GOP Front Runner Donald Trump, it was revealed that he would not rule out nuclear weapon usage for the fight between the United States and the Islamic State of Iraq and Syria, more commonly known as the ISIS. When asked if Trump would give consideration for nuclear retaliation after the attacks in Brussels, he answered saying that he would not rule it out but wouldn't say even if he was going to as he wanted them to be in doubt whether US will use nuclear weaponry. He elaborated saying that the country needs to be unpredictable for the enemy.

When he was asked whether he would have used the country's nuclear capability after the incident on September 11, Trump said that he would have, but only as the last resort. While we stay worried and bound by laws, the ISIS is beheading and drowning people, he said. Trump highlighted that we are not taking any proper action towards the terrorism we face. He also added concerns that the Middle Eastern Muslims don't respect the US.

Donald Trump also proposed at a gathering that the involvement of the US with NATO international alliance should be rethought and this received much criticism from Republicans. He explained saying that NATO is obsolete and helps other countries over us.

Trump on weakness of the country borders

The Republican frontrunner, Donald J. Trump addressed a large gathering of his supporters at the Wright Brothers Aero hanger. The huge crowd gathered to capacity of the hanger chanted "Build the wall" when Trump arrived at the location. And to the cheers of the crowd Trump responded saying that we will build the wall and Mexico will pay for it.

Someone in the audience made a move towards the presidential candidate by the end of the event and the security instantly surrounded Trump. The address was continued by Trump after the incident and he asked the crowd whether there is anything more fun than one of his rallies.

On a more serious note, he said that there were several issues in the country like the jobs of the citizens being sucked away, military being unable to defeat the ISIS, comparing the US borders to Swiss cheese. He took this moment an opportunity to express his 100% support to waterboarding, an enhanced interrogation technique.

The event flowed smoothly with no major issues unlike the recent Chicago Trump rally which was cancelled because of protestors.

Trump also took time to go against his challengers like Senators Marco Rubio and Ted Cruz. He said that Ted Cruz lifts up the bible and then puts it down and les. He also talked of Gov. John Kasich disproving of his activity at the Lehman Brothers and for his NAFTA vote in 1990s as a congressmen. Trump said that Kasich is not tough enough and is a baby who can't be president.

Terrorist interrogation

Donald Trump further explained his take on waterboarding and other enhancements of interrogation methods by directly saying "Torture Works". He also said that he would bring back interrogation techniques which are much worse than waterboarding, at a Q&A session in Sun City, S.C.

Trump's belief as he explained was that these interrogation methods would eradicate or lessen the terrorism which is a threat to the United States. He made clear that this is not old times where people engaged in hand to hand combat and mentioned that the country is in danger from criminals and terrorists holding highly destructive weapons that could even end the world.

In a USA Today op-ed Trump expressed that he would support these enhanced techniques of interrogation if it would secure the safety of the country. Although Senator Ted Cruz said he would do the same in such a situation, he also said that he doesn't share the same beliefs about the liberal application of such techniques.

Another US Senator John McCain responded to Trump indirectly at a Senate floor speech saying that his statements may mislead the citizens about how the US government gathers intelligence and defends security. He also expressed concerns that these statements must not go unanswered as they may change the idea of people about what we are fighting for and the type of nation we stand as.

#MAKEAMERICAGREATAGAIN

Veterans

Trump says 300,000 Veterans "kicked The Bucket" While Awaiting VA care

The Republican presidential candidate, Donald Trump announced his intention of fixing "destruction" at the department of Veterans Affairs. He said this at the U.S Navy fortress. Trump gave alarm about the appalling current state of the department of Veterans Affairs. He said this in a rally at USS Wisconsin. He added that over 300,000 veterans gave up the ghost on the process of waiting for care. Trump's statement in this regard emanated from the September 2 report by the VA's office that unveiled that the agency's record was deficient. This article attempts to examine Trump's claim.

First, an investigation portrayed that the reporter complained about the provision of unfinished services at the VA. The investigation was based on the agency's Health Eligibility Center which is described as authoritative to the veterans. A report as at Sept.30, 2014 showed that the status given to the VA was incomplete because of lack of information flow. The report signifies that there is basis for Trump's number but the figure remained confusing and complex. Also, the agency's enrollment database commenced in 1998 which encompasses awaiting files but the report was not specific about the member. The Inspector later observed that there was a veteran that died in 1988 but was still shortlisted in the pending 2014 VA application showing the degree of inaccuracy.

Specifically, Trump promised to repair and renovate the VA following over 300,000 veterans who died, which he posited. But the fact remains that Trump's figure could be disputed since he went beyond what the Inspector was able to conclude.

John McCain has 'done nothing' for The Retired Military

The Republican Candidate Donald Trump, has alleged that John McCain had done completely nothing for the Veteran. The GOP front runner said this on July 19 2015. He expressed disappointment over his alleged less concerned attitude, that McCain has continued to show the vets. Trump said he had always shown an indefatigable concern to the veterans. He however, pointed that the Vets were in severe suffering. The billionaire promised to fight for the veterans whom he said, had been abandoned by McCain and his Senate colleagues. He expressed pity, over 1,000 veterans that died while waiting for medical care. The question as to whether McCain cares or not to fellow veterans is the issue of discussion in this article.

According to McCain's office, in June 2015, McCain sponsored the amendment to National Defense Authorization Act of 2016 as to compensate for the travel expenses for the families of troops killed in overseas mission, He also introduced the Clay Hunt Suicide Prevention for American Veterans, McCain, employed five caseworkers as to assisting veterans Who are running into problems at the department of Veterans Affairs. According to the report also, McCain also reached out veterans group at every time.

Donald Trump, in his response to a statement made against him that McCain had been fixing and reforming the VA, said he had no idea of it. He further said that if he did, he would have known that McCain had been trying to give veterans good health and hold VA accountable for his disservice.

Leader of the New York veterans' group defend Donald

Since Donald Trump commented against Sen. John McCain, antagonists and protagonists had always surrounded him. Fortunately enough, the leader of the veterans residing at New York, however supported Trump. He said unequivocally that Trump had never portrayed a bad character or attitude on them. He therefore, added that, the GOP front runner had been with them right from the inception of the organization in 1983.He therefore pointed that, if it were not Trump, the project at lower Manhattan would not have been accomplished. He added that, Trump also, committed $1M fund which enabled the property downtown offered by Koch administration to be actualized.

In another development, Trump on Saturday in a Family Leadership Council summit at Iowa said McCain was only a war hero since he was apprehended, tortured and held captive as a POW in Vietnam for over 5years.

In a recent development also, Donald, in response to McCain's demand for apology, said he owed him no apology and so refused to render any apology to him. Trump said this on a Sunday in July 2015, when he was addressing ABC's Martha Raddatz. He said, he would insist on what he had been saying and would never render any apology to McCain whom he had accused of doing nothing for the veterans. Trump added that he had examined the veterans in his campaign trail, they are suffering, McCain has done nothing for them, he said. The GOP front runner added that, the record of his help to the veteran was still well documented. I served as a co-chairman of the New York Vietnam Veterans Memorial Commission and was responsible, with a small group, for getting it built, he said.

The leader of the New York veteran group however, supported and recalled how Trump helped a retired Sargent with $10,000 dollars to start his education.

#MAKEAMERICAGREATAGAIN

References

"Donald Trump Biography." - Childhood, Life Achievements & Timeline. Web. 06 June 2016.

"Donald Trump Biography." - Family, Childhood, Children, Parents, Story, Wife, School, Information, Born, College, Contract. Web. 06 June 2016.

"Donald Trump." Bio.com. A&E Networks Television. Web. 06 June 2016.

MacNeal, Caitlin. "Trump Clarifies Position On Foreign Worker Visas After Debate." TPM. 04 Mar. 2016. Web. 06 June 2016.

"Trump Backs Waterboarding and 'a Lot More' after Brussels Attacks." NewsTalk 610 KDAL AM. 22 Mar. 2016. Web. 06 June 2016.

Reports, Money Morning Staff. "How Did Trump Do in the Debate?" Money Morning We Make Investing Profitable. 11 Nov. 2015. Web. 06 June 2016.

Byrnes, Jesse. "Trump: NBC 'stands behind Brian Williams,' Not People Who Tell It 'like It Is'"TheHill. 29 June 2015. Web. 06 June 2016.

Costa, Robert. "In New Hampshire, Trump's Pitch Is Urgent and His Schedule Full." Washington Post. The Washington Post, 04 Feb. 2016. Web. 06 June 2016.

Woodall, Candy. "'Oh, We're Gonna Build the Wall,' Donald Trump Says to Loud Cheers in Harrisburg." PennLive.com. 21 Apr. 2016. Web. 06 June 2016.

Condon, Stephanie. "In 10th GOP Debate, Marco Rubio Steps up to the Plate against Donald Trump."CBSNews. CBS Interactive, 26 Feb. 2016. Web. 06 June 2016.

Selby, Gardner. " Ted Cruz ad, assailed by Trump, leaves out Trump's declared shift on abortion." PolitiFact Texas. 17 Feb. 2016. Web. 06 June 2016.

Hensch, Mark. "Trump Not Sure about past Donations to Planned Parenthood." TheHill. 16 Aug. 2015. Web. 06 June 2016.

Ehrenfreund, Max . "I Asked Psychologists to Analyze Trump Supporters. This Is What I Learned."Washington Post. The Washington Post, 15 Oct. 2015. Web. 06 June 2016.

Bahadur, Nina. "Donald Trump Gets Womansplained On Planned Parenthood." Huffington Post. N.p., 09 Oct. 2015. Web. 6 June 2016.

Baxley, Jaymie. "In Fayetteville, Trump Vows to Restore Lost N.C. Jobs." Richmond County Daily Journal. 10 Mar. 2016. Web. 06 June 2016.

Scott, Eugene. "Trump: Arm Teachers to Stop School Massacres." CNN. Cable News Network, 03 Oct. 2015. Web. 06 June 2016.

"Election 2016: Donald Trump." CBSNews. CBS Interactive, 22 Dec. 2015. Web. 06 June 2016.

"Donald Trump, New Gun Plan: Nationwide Concealed Carry, Remove Bans On All Guns, Fix Mental Health Problem." Headlines Global News RSS. 19 Sept. 2015. Web. 06 June 2016.

Gorman, Michelle. "WHO'S THE BEST REPUBLICAN CANDIDATE WITH A GUN?" News Week. 29 Feb. 2016. Web. 06 June 2016.

"Trump, Clinton Battle for Israel Vote, Vow Support in Major Washington Speeches | Fox News." Fox News. FOX News Network, 21 Mar. 2016. Web. 06 June 2016.

"Trump At AIPAC: 'I Didn't Come Here Tonight To Pander To You About Israel'"CBS New York. 21 Mar. 2016. Web. 06 June 2016.

Garcia, Catherine. "Trump, Cruz, Rubio Argue over Who Supports Israel the Most." The Week. 25 Feb. 2016. Web. 06 June 2016.

Burgess, Anna. "Trump Sends Sparks Flying in Worcester." - Lowell Sun Online. 19 Nov. 2015. Web. 06 June 2016.

Cornbluh, Jacob. "Trump Thinks President Obama Hates Israel | Nation." Jewish Journal News. 29 Oct. 2015. Web. 06 June 2016.

"Trump: 'I Would Love To See A Michael Bloomberg Run'" NBC News. 24 Jan. 2016. Web. 06 June 2016.

McIntosh, David. "Club for Growth: Trump's Economic Policies Put Him in Liberal Mainstream."Washington Post. The Washington Post, 22 Sept. 2015. Web. 06 June 2016.

Marans, Daniel. "Donald Trump's Big Socialist Idea." Huffington Post. 26 Feb. 2016. Web. 6 June 2016.

Aron, Michael. "Six-Year Anniversary of the Affordable Care Act | Video | NJTV News." NJTV News. 23 Mar. 2016. Web. 06 June 2016.

MacNeal, Caitlin. "Donald Trump Releases Health Care Plan To Replace Obamacare." TPM. 03 Mar. 2016. Web. 06 June 2016.

Trump: Some GOPers Would See a Person Dying Outside a Hospital and Say 'Let 'Em Die'." Mediaite. 1 Feb. 2016. Web. 06 June 2016.

Elliot, Philip. "Why Donald Trump Is Turning on John Kasich." Time. Time, 14 Mar. 2016. Web. 06 June 2016.

Thibodeau, Patrick. "Donald Trump, Zingers and All, Emerges as Sharp H-1B Critic." Computerworld. 16 Aug. 2015. Web. 06 June 2016.

Parker, Ashley. "What You Missed in the Debate." The New York Times. The New York Times, 10 Mar. 2016. Web. 06 June 2016.

Dingle, Stephon. "Donald Trump Wants 'surveillance of Certain Mosques'." Alabama News Weather Sports Traffic. 21 Nov. 2015. Web. 06 June 2016.

McCammon, Sarah. "Trump Opponents Try To Build Property Rights Into A S.C. Primary Issue."KGOU. 17 Feb. 2016. Web. 06 June 2016.

Wong, Curtis. "Gay YouTube Personality 'Comes Out' In Support Of Donald Trump." Huffington Post. 28 Oct. 2015. Web. 6 June 2016.

Tani, Maxwell. "Here Are the Best Moments from the GOP Debate." Business Insider. Business Insider, Inc, 06 Feb. 2016. Web. 06 June 2016.

Lewis, Philip. "Donald Trump On Climate Change: 'I Believe It Goes Up And It Goes Down'." Huffington Post. 22 Sept. 2015. Web. 6 June 2016.

Glaun, Dan. "UMass Police Union Disavows Parent Union's Endorsement of Donald Trump." Masslive.com. 18 Dec. 2015. Web. 06 June 2016.

Santucci, John. "Experts Doubt Donald Trump's Plan to Execute Cop Killers Would Pass Muster." ABC News. ABC News Network, 17 Dec. 2015. Web. 06 June 2016.

Jacobson, Louis. "What Donald Trump Said about the Chinese Inventing the 'hoax' of Climate Change." Politifact. 24 Jan. 2016. Web. 06 June 2016.

Farrell, Paul B. "Donald Trump's USA Inc. Will Kill Our Climate, Our Economy and Our Democracy." MarketWatch. 25 Aug. 2015. Web. 06 June 2016.

Dunbar, John. "Small Businesses for Trump: 'Just Get Somebody Different in There'" Center for Public Integrity. 25 Feb. 2016. Web. 06 June 2016.

Berenson, Tessa. "Trump Tries His Hand at Retail Politics in New Hampshire." Time. Time, 8 Feb. 2016. Web. 06 June 2016.

Neff, Blake. "Trump Slams US Public Schools, Pledges To Kill Common Core [VIDEO]." The Daily Caller. 26 Jan. 2016. Web. 06 June 2016.

Enloe, Chris. "Donald Trump Excoriates House Republicans Over Budget Deal: Republicans 'Threw the Towel In, Showed No Budget Discipline'." The Blaze. 18 Dec. 2015. Web. 06 June 2016.

Milbank, Dana. "Dana Milbank: Donald Trump's 'Captain Underpants' Campaign." Investor's Business Daily. 26 Feb. 2016. Web. 06 June 2016.

Wise, Hannah. "Trump Speaks in MSNBC Town Hall to Counter Cruz, Rubio Appearance on CNN." Trail Blazers Blog. 17 Feb. 2016. Web. 06 June 2016.

Flores, Reena. "Donald Trump Open to Nuclear Retaliation after Brussels Attack." CBSNews. CBS Interactive, 24 Mar. 2016. Web. 06 June 2016.

Hulsey, Lynn. "Donald Trump Speaks to Thousands at Dayton Rally." Dayton Daily News. 13 Mar. 2016. Web. 06 June 2016.

Deaton, Chris. "Trump: 'Torture Works, OK Folks?'" Weekly Standard. 17 Feb. 2016. Web. 06 June 2016.

Fiske, Warran. "Trump Says 300,000 Veterans Died Waiting VA Care." Politifact. 09 Nov. 2015. Web. 06 June 2016.

Qiu, Linda. "After 'not a War Hero' Remark, Donald Trump Says John McCain Has 'done Nothing' for Veterans." Politifact. 21 July 2015. Web. 06 June 2016.

Santucci, John. "Leader of New York Veterans Group Defends Donald Trump." ABC News. ABC News Network, 20 July 2015. Web. 06 June 2016.

#MAKEAMERICAGREATAGAIN

#MAKEAMERICAGREATAGAIN

www.ingramcontent.com/pod-product-compliance
Lightning Source LLC
Chambersburg PA
CBHW020559030426
42337CB00013B/1147